Essence of Being

MIMI NOVIC

Aspiring Hope
Publishing

Copyright © Mimi Novic 2019

Cover images courtesy of stereohype/Shutterstock ©

Cover design by EMC Design Ltd

Design and typeset by EMC Design Ltd

All rights reserved. No part of this publication may be reproduced, stored in a retrieval system, or transmitted in any form or by any means, electronic, mechanical, photocopy, recording or otherwise, without prior written permission of the copyright owner. Nor can it be circulated in any form of binding or cover other than that in which it is published and without similar condition including this condition being imposed on a subsequent purchaser.

British Library Cataloguing Publication Data.

A catalogue record for this book is available from the British Library

ISBN 978-1-9999120-6-2

Published by Aspiring Hope Publishing

In the Name of God, the Most Beneficent, the Most Merciful

For my Beloved ones...

For you My Beloved friend Isa, who brought hope to my life, your kindness is the balm to my heart.

For you My Beloved friend Muhammad, your fountain of love waters my soul in love.

Forever grateful and may peace be upon your beautiful souls.

ABOUT THE AUTHOR

Mimi Novic is one of today's bestselling authors in the genre of inspirational, self help and spiritual books.

She is one of the most highly respected self-awareness teachers internationally, having won many awards for her work.

As well as being an inspirational author and life coach in the fields of self-development and spiritual growth, she runs clinics internationally using her expertise as a therapist, complementary medical practitioner and inspirational speaker.

Through Mimi's various ground-breaking healing techniques, many have learnt to gain wellness in mind, body and spirit as well as developing positive thinking techniques to gain greater freedom to achieve a more balanced and peaceful life.

She has specialised and devised various transformational healing methods, one of the most well known and widely used ones by therapists, as well as the public, is the breathing technique, called "Healing Breath Peaceful Soul" which is a method of deep meditation and awakening through the power of breath.

Through her work as a complementary medical practitioner, therapist, voiceover artist, author and motivational speaker, she encourages everyone, from whatever walk of life they may be from, to embark upon the journey of self-discovery, in order to heal their lives. Mimi teaches seminars and workshops in alternative medicine and self-awareness, as well as complementary and holistic therapies, working around the world in clinics, retreats and on a one to one basis.

Her thought provoking writings are also available as a series of meditation albums, which beautifully harmonise her inspirations with soul enlightening music, that awaken the heart and bring peace and serenity back into our lives. An expert in her field, Mimi continues to help people find their life's purpose, through her continuing motivational work.

It is the driving force behind the passion to help people realise their true potential and transform their life so that they may become fulfilled and gain the confidence and wellbeing to achieve their lifelong ambitions and heal from within.

FOREWORD

Within the deepest pools of the hidden sanctuary of the beauty that is us, rests the secret of life.

Our journey towards the infinite began when our soul first heard our name being called with the invitation to come and see the splendour of the earth.

Our life here is the temporary manifestation and appearance of only one ray of our real being, shining in all its splendour, for our divinity in all its glory exists in the ocean of reality.

All else on this earthly plane is a mirror and a reflection of the perpetual eternity that glorifies the exalted and praised Creator.

We have been invited upon this splendid voyage of discovery with all those we meet along the way, as they to have a part in this embroidery of the celestial promise to one another.

Let us become as one as we pass through the realms of the beautiful, the holy, the glorious and let us without reservation and with total abundance embrace the essence of our grace, leaving the scattered petals of the perfume of heaven along the way.

My soul is running through the desert in ecstasy searching for your touch,
My friend the wind has promised to take me where you sleep.
Listen this night, as I will whisper the secrets of a thousand lifetimes that we have shared.
Come and lay your gentle heartbeats beside me.

Rub your eyes, and look again with love at everything,
Do not ask what love can make or do,
Just look at you, that is what love can do.
You are all the colours of the world,
Every star is part of you,
And all of existence is waiting for you to discover it.

There are some who are so connected to us
and yet they are miles away from us,
Then there are others who are right beside us
and yet they are so far away.

We think we meet people by chance,
But we've been expecting one another a whole lifetime,
Just waiting for the galaxies to align and show us
the way to each other.

To reach happiness you do not need a map,
You need to follow your own soul.

It is not love that hurts, but the journey until it's found.

When hope whispers
"Let us begin again"
Take its hand and kiss the starlight.

If you only ever fill your heart with tears,
You will never be able to scatter the light
that drives away the darkness.

There was once a discussion between tears and smiles,
The tears said: "We yearn to be you,
because you are always happy".
And the smile replied: "That is not so, because too often,
it's so hard for me to hide your pain."

Every step I feel, in every road I take, I find you, as if you had never left, because your essence is in the air, and in every stone of the street, I hear the echoes of your voice.

As I close my eyes I am no longer here, nor there, nor anywhere, but you, oh you, are everywhere,

And I will spend the rest of my days looking for you.

This day, this hour, this minute, will not come around again in our entire life.

Let us speak with love to everyone we meet and remind each other how beautiful we really are.

𝓛ife is the biggest dance,
It all depends if we get up and enjoy the music.
Live, knowing that we do not know if
tomorrow we will have time.

Don't count the steps you've walked,
Nor the shoes you've worn, nor the pain you've felt,
nor how long it took you,
It only matters the footprints you've left
in the heart's you've met along the way.

There are some people that when we think about them,
They can transport us to a place,
They can transform our mood at once,
They can accompany us everywhere,
Even without their presence.

Those that tell us we are difficult to understand,
Are the ones who have lost the desire to discover us.
Walk away from everyone who can't see you,
And you will see yourself.

Your peace is more important than trying to understand why something happened the way it happened. Sometimes it is not a question of understanding, but of accepting.

𝓡ise above everything and listen to what your heart is guiding you to do.

The secret of peace…
Accept yourself in all your magnificent beauty.

There are some moments with some people
that are unrepeatable,
And it is for this,
We continue to live for.

It is the connection with the Divine energy that exists within all of us that teaches us how to harness our real power.

It is this long forgotten treasure that remains undiscovered that gives us the ability and opportunity to transform our lives within every aspect of our daily life.

*O*nce you know your worth,
You don't need to explain yourself to anyone.
Just keep walking along the open road until you meet those that recognise you,
This is where you belong.

If we truly believed in ourselves the opinions of others would never hold us prisoner.

There is no loneliness for the one who has made friends with their heart.

Never force anyone to stay.
Everyone is free to choose every day whether to stay or to go,
It is only when a person is totally free to choose and yet decides
to stay that you know your presence matters to their life.

*O*nly those who recognise and accept their own light, who tread with each footstep towards the dusty road of true love, are the unveiled ones who see and adore the light in others.

It's those souls we should take by the hand, as they have walked with the broken and fragile and know the treasure of compassion.

We can't walk towards love with anyone not heading in the same direction as us.

The one who doesn't try, never succeeds.
The one who doesn't risk, never wins.
The pain is inevitable.
The suffering is optional.
You will shed tears with or without those you miss.
Live intensely.
Do whatever it takes to keep that flame of passion for life burning inside.

For those who don't belong,
For those that don't fit in,
For those who are the dreamers and free spirits of the world,
Keep soaring above the earth,
You are the courageous ones who have discovered
your wings of freedom,
Now show everyone what touching the stars is all about.

Nothing and no one is a waste of time,
If it doesn't give us what we are looking for,
It teaches us what we need to learn.

In the end we are all just memories of those we met upon the shores of yesterday.

We are all thinking that no one understands us,
But what is important is that we understand ourselves.

There are some eyes we meet that are full of silence,
Yet they speak words that reach the depths of our being
that only our soul would understand.

Who touches your soul, stays with you forever,
Anyone and anything can make the heart beat faster,
But not everyone can make your soul quiver.

Smile, dream, don't give up.
Don't try to be like everyone else, it's impossible,
Be totally your extraordinary self,
Paint the world with the colours of your spirit.

You cannot shorten the road that you're meant
to travel on,
You know that everything along the way has a reason
and a season.
Embrace everyone, they are all here to teach us.
Let's chase the rainbows as long as they weave their magic
and guide us towards our destiny.

Dreams may come and dreams may go,
That is their beauty, to capture us, to make us chase them,
to make us fly to reach them,
And to never lose the desire to keep dreaming among
the brokenness,
Even if it's for one more day.

$\mathcal{W}$e either build walls between each other
through our misunderstandings,
Or we build bridges to reach other through our compassion.

Wounded souls feel the deepest feelings,
Understand the greatest sorrows,
And their life is a testimony to hope.

Sometimes it may seem that we are lost,
Instead we have have arrived exactly where the destination
is waiting for us.

If anything appears along your way, thank it,
That which doesn't arrive, you don't need it.

There are only two wonderful destinations that draw
a thousand emotions within each of us,
The heart and the soul,
Travel to each one in every moment.

There comes a time you almost do not ask
but when you have the courage to ask,
It changes your life.

Making a change in our life can be difficult,
But what is more difficult?
Regret.
To say to yourself one day:
"I'm suffering because I was too afraid to take a chance."

It is sometimes not explainable the yearnings that we feel that come over us like waves, stirring us, moving us, calling us to go somewhere, to do something yet we can't always understand the message.

Maybe it is because we are afraid, that we prevent the heart from speaking,

But it speaks to us whether we listen or not.

It whispers, it shouts, it trembles, it laments but always it's there trying to remind us of where it's trying to take us.

Those flutters you feel, listen to them

The answer to everything is love.
We are all searching for the same thing, if only we realised, oh how our hearts would hold hands.
If only we awakened and saw that we have no need to search.
It is because we are so far away from ourselves that we suffer.
If we stopped for a moment and turned around and saw that love was waiting with open arms for us all along.

Every soul has the essence of the Divine truth love within them.

Some sleep in this life, as this is their path, nothing can awaken them unless they themselves want to be awoken from the deep sleep of the soul.

Those that are awake must try in love and humbleness to awaken the sleeper, it is our duty to our fellow human being to extend the glory of the heavenly light within us, in this ever darkening world, but we must also accept that some prefer to sleep as their wounds are too painful and their heart too broken.

Ultimately, they will reach the final destination of Divine grace and love, where we will all be as one for eternity.

Each and every one of us has been given the book of our life before our birth and agreed to live it upon this earth and amongst the worlds, only we ourselves can read the pages of that book, it is not for anyone to see, it is between God and us.

None of us know what anyone else has promised the One who created us, we only know that we know nothing, other than that we all share the same heartache, the devastation of separation from our true reality and unless there was darkness we would never know light.

The light of our souls is never extinguished, it can never be, as the eternal One abides within each and every heart, forever.

Your flame flickers in the midnight light,
Your eyes yearning,
To be found by the one,
Who can touch the corners of your soul,
And caress the pain of the past,
Calling you to life again,
Waking every forgotten symphony that is still waiting
to be played.

The heart trembling,
Waiting for its strings to be strung to the music of love,
Longing in the darkness,
Embracing the moonlight,
Kissing its reflection in your face,
Adoring the beauty of your essence,
And then if one day your thoughts turn to the memory of us,
sometime, somewhere in this worldly realm,
Follow the trail of my tears,
As I will be waiting for you by the shores of the ocean of hope,
Singing to the wind, asking it to catch the stars and scatter
them at your feet,
Showing you the way back to me.

Don't ask me how long this moment will last,
Don't ask me if I will never forget you,
Don't ask if we have eternity,
Just take my hand and always remember,
That true love never dies,
And long after the roses have shed their fragrance,
And the moon has gone to dream,
I will be listening forever,
Waiting to hear your voice calling my name once more.

We are always either remembering the past or looking forward to the future,
Yet the only real place we stand that is real, is on the bridge of the now.

Above all else we have to be brave, be fearless, be open.
Accept yourself, your life, your scars, your mistakes.
Forget what people think, no one really knows the struggles of your past, nor tasted the salt of your tears.
It doesn't matter what the world believes about you, it's what you believe about yourself that matters.
Take a leap of faith, find what is holding you prisoner and let it go.

You are an ambassador of love.
Let your whole being
illuminate the world with its presence.

Sometimes the only way to find peace,
Is to stop asking the questions,
And instead listen to the answers within
whispering their wisdom.

Let's run with passion, love and hope,
To every place our heart takes us.

That's the beauty of falling in love,
The totally unexpected moment it arrives,
Taking us completely on a new road
that we've never travelled on.

Always be with the ones who stir your soul to soar above the clouds and catch the sunrise in your eyes.

As the echoes of yesterday, echo in the deepest chambers within our heart,
Our life journey unfolds every day before us.
As the memories fade,
The only one thing that matters is the ones that we loved and those who despite everything, loved us.

There is a secret way to find the answers,
It is not to travel far away, but to venture
deeper within ourselves.

And the Sublime hand that guides us towards our soul's purpose is the fountain of courage that already resides within us, ever whispering its messages of encouragement, calling us towards those destinations amongst the trail of stars that will illuminate our way to our real home.

*L*ife is but a fleeting moment, only a glimmer of our real essence is here upon this earth, the rest abides in the celestial realms, never leaving the glory of the Divine.

Our presence here is temporary, yet it is a continuous journey towards eternity.

For everything there is a time, for everything there is a season, and so for us.
We are not outside the sphere of God's great plan, we exist in an intricately sewn carpet of existence, each one of our souls gently caressing the moments of life of another, whether or not we have ever met, we each have a profound effect on each other's lives.

The flight of the soul is propelled by its yearning to be free of this physical world.
Within the essence of everyone's heart, exists the same ocean of love that encapsulates within in it endless tears of separation that pour infinitely upon the soul to water the gardens of loneliness.

We are all fragile beings, yet we are all belonging to the almighty Lord, so there is no separateness, ever, we are eternal.

And one day we shall all be together in the ocean of love and unity.

Until then we can only dream.

There are times we get lost along our journey and there is a reason for this also, sometimes it's inevitable.
Always there is wisdom to be gained during that time.

Adversity teaches us that any opportunity to gain insight into our deepest caverns of our soul is what builds strength and courage.
Learn from your mistakes, but most importantly, let them go.

Love makes us invincible…Always be in love
Life is not always about winning…It is about never surrendering.

When your heart is in peace,
Then you can be certain that you are exactly
where you should be,
Within this moment of destiny.

Those that capture our heart give us an extraordinary opportunity to set ourselves free of this earthly existence.

It's only when we cling to their physical appearance that our heart begins to feel tied down and misses the glorious moments that their soul is trying to teach us.

If we fly with their whispers that are beyond words, then the wind shall forever carry us and we shall be in a state of perpetual bliss, joined forever in the oceans of ecstasy.

*D*on't be afraid to let the tears fall,
They are the lights that shine upon our spirit,
Reminding us that we are so much more than we realise,
They wash our eyes with droplets from heaven,
So we may see that we are part of the celestial stardust
that sprinkles the earth with hope,
And each of us is a universe spinning constantly amongst
the realms of eternity.

Be so that everyone you meet is reminded by your presence to forever believe in love.

*L*ove has taken me by the hand and I don't know where it's taking me,
But wherever it is I know it is where I am longing to be.

I stand looking at the ocean of loneliness watching the passing ship of my life,
I whisper into the distance hoping that you will one day hear my call of love.
My light still flickers wishing that upon your lips is still my name and one day you will remember me and come and take me into your arms.
But if destiny hasn't written my name upon your heart,
Then I will stand always at the edge of this lifetime waiting for your hands to wipe away my tears that are the mirror of your soul.

We are just fragments of a moment,
Each whirling in ecstatic dance looking for each other
in the mists of time,
Running through the streets of loneliness,
Searching for joy to hold our hand,
For love to whisper our name,
Calling us to where we belong, in each other's arms,
once again.

There are moments that are unrepeatable with anyone else other than with the one who took the journey to walk to the furthest door along the corridors that led to the caverns of your tears,

Who wiped the sorrow from your brow and caressed the teardrops as they silently fell into the pool of yesterday.

Acceptance of our real being is the key that unlocks the mystical pathways to the ever gracious celestial worlds,

Where we are in total union with the sacred and holy manifestation of the Creator; where the reason for our existence came into being from pre eternity towards the never ending rivers of paradise that water our gracious and tender spirit.

We may meet so many people along this long road,
But it is of no use,
Until we finally meet ourselves.

We took our whole lifetime for messages to help us
understand our existence and yet we forget,
Our life is our message.

Taking the journey towards ourselves is the hardest journey we have to make in this life and the most courageous, but when we finally embark upon it, the awakenings and enlightening moments it brings are beyond the description of words and worlds, everything becomes felt and lived with the soul's guidance.

Our life is never the same again.

What we once saw with our eyes, we can only see now with our heart, all else disappears into the past, of a life we once lived.

To be of service to others, is to serve our own soul, there is no greater love than the one we have been created with and that is the Divine spark within all of us.

There are rare beings that we meet along this journey that are able to light this wondrous and mystical flame within us, as they see what is hidden to most and it's these ones that are sent to help us along our true life path that teach us the greatest lessons; find them, they are always somewhere where you least expect.

$\mathcal{O}$ur time and life is precious and what we share with others is important, as we are exchanging moments of our life with the other person, which we will never get back, cherish this and honour and protect it, we must choose wisely who to spend our golden seconds with and with whom to share our presence with.

What we do with new found openings is up to us and that is the gift of free will, destiny hides its secrets though.

It is through enlightenment and hope that whatever it is your soul is seeking, you will find in this lifetime and beyond.

Be with those that give you the wind of hope and believe in your spirit, you will recognise them easily as there is a certain unexplainable peace and exhilaration you will feel when you are with them and a delicateness of love that will touch your heart like never before.

Don't listen to anything other than your own soul.

On the preserved tablet of destiny we were each presented with the book of our life before we placed our footsteps on earth, sometimes in the dimly lit nights of this world, we can read what we promised each other.

𝓛et us not forget for one single moment that
everyone we meet has a story to tell.
We all have hearts that have been broken,
Wings that have been injured,
And dreams that no longer fly.

I hope that we will never be late.
Too late to love, too late to forgive, too late to hug, too late to sing a song, too late to dance, too late to hold hands, too late to say… Please stay, there's so much more of me, of you, of us.
Don't let us ever be too late.

Don't allow anyone to make you feel like you are
not good enough,
Allow yourself the space and time to heal your hurting heart, to wipe the tears of lost memories, to understand all those unresolved thoughts.
Sometimes all that's necessary and needed is to take a distance from everything,
So that we can find that place within us that we've never been to before.

𝓛et people feel comfortable with you so that they can truly be themselves,
Let them be open, free, raw, fragile, real.
The world needs so much more of this liberating compassion.

*O*ur heart's invite us to meet one another, long before
our bodies actually meet,
They have a secret way of singing a song that calls all those
that recognise its music to hear the invitation,
At exactly the right time that we are needed
in each other's lives.

Never be less than you are.
You have a unique contribution to make to this world.

Slow down and enjoy the journey right now.
Take time for the people in your life.
Take time to look around and enjoy the experience of living.
Nothing stays the same and won't always be there.
Appreciate it all while it rests in your hands.

Choose to see the world through your heart
instead of your eyes,
There is a magnificence in its view.

Compassion begins when we realise that we are all struggling in our own way.

The conversations we have with ourselves have a tremendous power over us.
They affect our body, our mind, our mood and everything we do.
Every waking moment is lived by our thoughts and therefore every one of them has a consequence.

*O*ur tears are the mirror in which we see each other's spirit reflecting its desires.

Whatever situation and whatever person you're facing.
Always ask:
Is this bringing me closer to my heart?
Is this bringing me peace?
Is this allowing me the freedom to be the real me?
Is there love in the equation?
If the answer is no, respect yourself enough to walk away and travel towards everything that cherishes your being.

When we realise that everything is temporary,
We begin to feel less disappointed and we become more awake.
Seeing that the whole universe is working through us and
expressing itself with every step we take.

Each one of us holds the book of our life in our hands.
Every person we meet, walks into our life at the right chapter.
Sometimes we find out the reason at the end of the chapter, sometimes at the end of the book and sometimes in another lifetime.
What matters only is that we welcome every chance encounter as a lesson, a blessing.
For without these destined meetings we would be unable to know the purpose of our life.

𝓔 very heartbeat plays to its own rhythm.
Sometimes life brings us an opportunity to meet the ones that can hear its music and dance the dance of our soul.

Accept every invitation that takes you to where your heart and soul get excited to feel exhilaration and joy.

And despite everything that happens in the world
You have been given a whole lifetime…Just for you.

People's light travels faster than their words.
Don't look at what someone says to you.
Look at how they make you feel in their presence.

Wherever you are,
Bring your magic to that place.
Be the spark that ignites the passion for all those that meet you,
Even if only for a breath.

We are not just one insignificant piece of a jigsaw.
We are the whole part of a bigger picture, a bigger reason,
a greater plan.
That is why we must cry our tears, endure the suffering, touch
the joy, take the chance, trust in love,
And then look up to the skies, sing our song and dance our
dance and understand that is life, and it only happens once.

Take time away from the world.
Go to that secret place where no one knows that is hidden
inside of you and leave your burdens at the door.
Remember that no one can give you anything,
Unless you are first willing to give to yourself.

$\mathscr{O}$verthinking, over judging, over expecting, so many things are in excess these days, everything seems empty of truth and full of false facades.

What is real doesn't require anything more than accepting ourselves.

Simple truth is just to love, to live, to be with those that care for you, want you in their life, who are travelling towards the same destination, all else and everyone else let go of.

Love yourself enough to never settle for anything that disrespects your being.

Shatter the illusions and become all that you are.

pend your time only with those that celebrate your life.

*R*emain calm.
Everything that is happening right now is bringing you closer to knowing yourself.

Never forget those that lifted you from the shadows and walked beside you until you saw the light.

It has taken every step you have ever taken
to bring you here where you are now.

Time is never lost, its wisdom is to bring you to
where you need to be to learn what is necessary,

So that you can fulfil your destiny as you walk
and kiss the moon.

The soul is always awaiting the call of the heart and sits at the door of love hoping to catch a glimpse of its beloved.

When was the last time you asked your heart to show you the way.

We think we meet someone with our eyes,
Yet we actually meet them with our soul

Some special ones appear when we least expect it to help us
to remember to ignore the noise and listen to the music.
To remind us that there are angels everywhere that appear
in many forms,
Waiting for us to be ready to hear again how beautiful we are.

*O*ur life is neither too short, nor too long.
What matters is whether we use the time while we are here
to truly be part of everything,
Welcoming open heartedly and completely the journey
wherever it takes us.
As time is just the passage through eternity.

We have an internal compass that points us away
from people that are not right for us,
And points us towards the people that we feel good with.
It's trusting that unique pendulum within us,
That will bring us balance always.

Sometimes we have to walk barefoot on the ground,
Feel the raindrops upon our face,
Dance in the wind,
Sit and listen to the silence,
Let our soul rest a little,
And lift our eyes and gaze at infinity.

The only way to respect ourselves is to walk away from everything and everyone that doesn't honour our soul.

Sometimes we don't know why we meet the people we do, until they leave our lives.

Sometimes we share our life with people and yet never really know them or ever truly meet them.

Yet sometimes we may be with someone for only moments of our life and feel as if we have known them a lifetime.

Their arrival in our lives shows us what was missing within ourselves.

Their departure leaves only a deep sense of loss and we know no one else can ever fill the emptiness.

We spend too much time with those that never touch our heart, ignite our spirit, or make us feel alive, yet those that we love, we hardly see and our encounters with them last less than the glimpse of a tear drop.

We stand looking at the mirror of ourselves and do not recognise the eyes filled with tears that hide the oceans of separation.

We search for the winds of destiny, yet they are the breath that we breathe.

We look for the limitless horizons that carry us towards forever, yet the vista of forgetfulness falls like dust upon us making us forget who we are.

We stand on the bridge of yesterday and the fountains of our past empty themselves into the reflections of the forgotten dreams we once dreamt as children and the light of our hopes begin to fade.

We do not awaken, until the shadows fall upon the valley of sorrow and we are stirred only by the crumbling of the walls that we have built around our hearts and we ask the ever unanswered question;

Where did our life go and to whom did we give it to?

Unless we know the value of our ourselves,
How can anyone else value us.

It is pointless trying to convince your mind of something that your heart doesn't agree with.

When was the last time you opened the door to yourself and looked inside for the answers.

Everyone we meet brings with them all their happiness, sadness, regrets, tears, hopes, joys, wishes, yearnings,
And sometimes in between all of those chapters, we meet someone who can read the unspoken feelings,
We are all beautiful fragments of magic,
Weaving the hearts together of those who we meet along the way.

Everyone we meet has wounds upon their heart. Everyone is waiting for someone to scatter the seeds of love amongst their tears and to be patient enough to wait for their beautiful fragrance of dreams to awaken once more.

You will immediately know the people
that energise your soul,
As you will feel peace and joy after spending time with them.

In some people's embrace,
We are taught how to fly.

We may think sometimes that we are alone
because we are difficult to love.
But that is not the reason,
It is that it's difficult for most people to find
the road to our heart.

Always say yes to a new adventure,
a new journey, a new feeling.
Anything that takes you somewhere where
you've never been before always opens up
endless and beautiful possibilities.

In this heart sleep a thousand dreams,
Waiting to be awoken by the one who knows how to touch
the universes of divinity within me,
Guiding me to the hemispheres of eternal bliss.

And here I stand alone now without you by my side.
I have waited a whole lifetime to be with you.
Yet you have flown home now and here I am in the sea of my tears longing for your touch once more.
Knowing that the silent whispers of our love remind me in every fluttering heartbeat that somewhere beyond time and space the realms of the ethereal await our reunion.

There are some incredible souls who can
touch us so deeply,
Even though they have never held us in their arms,
Their spirit moves through us in such a way,
That they ignite a love, that becomes eternal.

Never be afraid of leaving everything.
If it's not taking you along the road towards your dreams.
Sometimes being alone gives us the space to walk through new doors, explore new ways and embrace new people.
Breathe in the sky and spread your wings.

There are times when it is better to be with those that understand our silence,
Then those that hear our words.

*Don't waste your time.
Everything that passes never returns.
We do not even own our own breath.
For every breath we take, we give one back.
Put your hand on your heart and honour your heartbeats.
It is through this connection that we enter the gateway to remembering that our life has a purpose, even if for a fleeting moment.*

Some rare people keep the secret key to our heart.
We only have to be brave enough to let them open the door
and come into our life.

Each one of us that arrives in this world has come for a reason.

We are so powerful beyond our wildest imagination.

Every single one of our footsteps is unique that it leaves a lasting imprint in the hearts of everyone we meet.

Every single one of us matters in this world.
When we respect and have real regard for ourselves and our own uniqueness.
Our light and power leaves everyone more joyful for meeting us.

Whatever happens...Be true to you,
So little by little we can bring a piece of heaven to each other.

Each and every one of our soul's thirsts for love,
Sadly we forget that the only fountain that can quench it,
Resides deep inside us.

When we begin to truly, deeply, love ourselves,
The whole world embraces us.

Some people make a difference to our life by just walking in and embracing us.

The spring of love flows from our heart and it's there that all the most beautiful of everything that exists can be found.

Awe inspiring moments, adventures, experiences are ready and waiting for us.
We just have to be courageous enough to embrace them whenever we receive their invitations.

Grab the magic, the joy, the excitement of loving
and living wherever you can find it and be only
with those who help you feel it.
It doesn't matter if it lasts a minute, a week, a month, a year,
Just hold it in your hands for as long as you can.
Memories last a lifetime.

Never lose your sense for wonder.
Everything we experience and everyone we meet is a door to another world, calling us to explore.
It is in between all this, that we find the adventures.

You are amazing and beautiful do you see that?
You have so much to give, don't hide anymore.
Focus on this moment and let go of all the burdened years of fears.
You've awoken to another sunrise this morning,
Cherish this place where you are now,
Another opportunity, another memory in the making.

𝓛et us not build walls with our words,
Let us stay silent and speak in a language that only our hearts can understand.

Every day magic and beauty awaits us,
When we look with the eyes of love.

Each day we decide, will today be a burden or
a wonderful opportunity.
It begins and ends with your thinking.
Sometimes we have no control over events but we have a choice
how to embrace what arrives.
Choice is everything, and we are the only ones
who can make it.

There are people,
That give you the freedom to feel excited, nervous and happy all at the same time.

They engrave their kisses on your soul.

They appear like the spring that awakens every sleeping flower inside of you and soothe the waves of longing of long forgotten dreams,

And a single touch soothes every painful wound left open from the past.

Life changes, revolves, there are always hurdles,
stops and detours, before we arrive at our destination.
But always the way continues even without our permission,
giving lessons,
Nothing is in vain, nothing is a waste of time.
So let us not just sit and let it pass by,
Let us grab the opportunity to be carried
by the wind of change,
It is where new horizons begin.

We know when we are with the right people,
When our heart feels the freedom to be itself.

𝓑e with the ones that make you feel the wind of hope
and believe in your spirit.

It is the words that are not said that speak the loudest,
It is the tears that fall in secret, that are the mirrors and
windows of our spirit.

Trust what you feel…There are so many ways the heart speaks to us.

We must never allow people to make us a prisoner
by what their opinion is about us,
What others think of us doesn't define us.
It's what we know of ourselves that keeps us free.

The sweetest, most unforgettable moments
that touch us in the deepest ways,
Always happen when we least expect them.

We have all felt that feeling of fluttering wings inside of us,
When your heart suddenly skips a beat,
When you feel an overwhelming sense of serenity, certainty
and excitement all at the same time,
That is when we need to listen closely,
As that is our heart telling us someone important
has just arrived in our life.

Eventually all that matters is that whatever we do and wherever we go…Our heart is in peace.

We have no control over what life may bring us,
But we have total power over what we bring to life.

When the world and all its noise becomes too much,
Take your yourself away, find your balance, take your rest,
go to that sanctuary within,
And when you feel ready again,
Continue dancing towards your dreams.

Infinite possibilities begin to arrive when we open
a space within us.
By letting go and forgiving,
Everything unresolved no longer has a hold on us,
And thus we set ourselves free.

Every experience has a lesson for us.

$\mathcal{O}$ur life is a reflection of the decisions we make.

Do whatever it takes that gives you even a single moment of happiness.
Hold hands with the feeling that makes you want to kiss the moon.

There are some who with one look understand us.
There are some who without us speaking a word,
know how we feel.
There are some who remind us of the melody our heart is
singing, when we momentarily lose our way.
And then there are some who give us what we need,
without us even having to ask them.
It is these ones that hold the mirror for us
to remember who we are.

Sometimes when we feel lonely,
We think we must be with people to fill that void.
But what we need instead is to be with the ones who give us
the space to be ourselves.

We never know what we are capable of enduring, creating,
achieving, making a difference,
Unless we take a step forward and try.

Sometimes you just have to pack up all the tears, all the sorrow, all the hurt, all the regrets and forgive yourself for not loving yourself sooner.
And then close the door of the cage of the past,
Fly towards another beginning,
While life calls your name with its sweet and tender kisses.

The beauty of being yourself,
There's no greater love you can give to the world.

𝒪ur life depends on our choices and our perception of things. Only we can decide how we see things and what we decide to do with those choices.

The further we travel from everything,
The closer we are to ourself.

This is your life no one else's.
All you have to do is live your story.
Don't let your light become dim by looking to the past with regret, it's gone, gone forever.
Let go of blame, forgive yourself.
Instead, listen to the beat of your heart, still beating, still having a purpose, and go and do whatever ignites your inner flame.

*D*on't let anyone overcrowd your spirit
and make you feel trapped.
Be with the ones who give space to your precious wings,
who lift your whole being,
So it can soar above the winds.

Take time to nurture and plant love in the garden of your soul.

There is no way in the world that anyone that anyone can show us where happiness is.
We can't hope for it to meet us somewhere, nor is it waiting for us to reach it.
We can only keep walking, keep yearning, keep being present in this very second.
The enchantment happens in the here, in this place we stand, in this very moment.
Life is about living in the now,
That's where the unearthed treasures remain hidden,
Longing to be found.

Everything and everyone has its season and time within existence.

𝒟on't be afraid of leaving everything,
If it's not taking you along the road towards your dreams.
Being alone gives us the space to walk through new doors,
explore new ways and embrace new people.
Breathe in the sky and spread your wings.

$\mathcal{O}$h brave ones you were made for far more beautiful things.
Adventure happens when it is shared with those who share our love of life.
Take the hands of those who gaze upon the same horizon as you, yet take you in different directions to reach the sunrise.
Be with those who scatter the stars at your feet and watch the moonlight write love songs upon your face.

$\mathcal{O}$ur whole life is a message to the world.
Everything we do is a mirror of our inner self.
Everything we think and say sends a message to everyone around us.
If we respect ourselves, if we make peace with our past and let it go,
Our presence begins to embrace each soul that we meet with love.
We all echo within each other's hearts forever,
Whether it's a thought, a memory, a smile, a feeling, a sigh,
Eventually we all become part of the symphony of each other's heartbeats.

www.ingramcontent.com/pod-product-compliance
Lightning Source LLC
Chambersburg PA
CBHW060356080526
44583CB00012B/348